Airs, Duetts, Trios, Etc. In The New Pantomime Of The Choice Of Harlequin: Or The Indian Chief

Michael Arne

In the interest of creating a more extensive selection of rare historical book reprints, we have chosen to reproduce this title even though it may possibly have occasional imperfections such as missing and blurred pages, missing text, poor pictures, markings, dark backgrounds and other reproduction issues beyond our control. Because this work is culturally important, we have made it available as a part of our commitment to protecting, preserving and promoting the world's literature. Thank you for your understanding.

AIRS, DUETTS, TRIOS, &c.

IN THE

NEW PANTOMIME

OF

The Choice of Harlequin:

OR,

The INDIAN CHIEF,

PERFORMED AT THE

THEATRE ROYAL

IN

COVENT-GARDEN.

LONDON:
Printed for T. CADELL, in the Strand.
M.DCC.LXXXI.

PRICE SIX-PENCE.

CHARACTERS.

Harlequin, - - Mr. BATES.

Keeper of Bridewell, - Mr. EDWIN.

Lieutenant, - - Mr. DARLY.

Groom Porter, - - Mr. DOYLE.

Clown, - - - Mr. STEVENS.

Virtue, - - - Mrs. MARTYR.

Pleasure, - - Mrs. MORTON.

SONGS, &c.

IN THE

NEW PANTOMIME

CALLED

The Choice of Harlequin.

RECITATIVE.

VIRTUE, (speaking to Harlequin.)

ARISE!—behold, commiſſion'd from above,
I come, th' immortal miniſter of Jove:
Let VIRTUE guide thy inexperienc'd youth,
And lead thy footſteps to the paths of truth.

AIR.

Let not pain or toil diſmay thee,
Faſhion rule, or vice betray thee;
Guilty pleaſures cannot laſt,
Crackling thorns are quickly paſt;

Flash with momentary fire,
Blaze awhile, and soon expire:
Solid joys unmix'd with woe,
Virtue only can bestow.

RECITATIVE.

PLEASURE, (to Harlequin.)

Turn thee from that brow austere,
A fairer form invites thee here;
Tun'd to notes of softest measure,
Listen to the voice of pleasure.

RECITATIVE.

VIRTUE.

Beyond that steep ascent and rugged path,
Where hangs yon dreadful precipice, uplift
Thy wond'ring eye, and on that height sublime
Behold my temple, fill'd with demi-gods,
And heroes fam'd of old!—if thou hast strength
To climb with me, a life of endless bliss
And wreaths immortal shall reward thy toil.

RECITATIVE.

PLEASURE.

From threat'ning rocks and dreary prospects turn
Thy frighted eye to level paths that court
Thy willing feet, where wreath'd with many a
    flower,
With odorous shrubs and scatter'd roses strew'd,
Uprises fair, the palace of delight.

DUETT.

VIRTUE.
List not to her flattering tale.

PLEASURE.
Let my friendly voice prevail.

VIRTUE.
Make my temple still thy home.

PLEASURE.
Hither, hither, hither come.

VIRTUE.
Sons of Fortune, come and see.

BOTH.
Follow, follow, follow me.

AIR.

AIR.

PLEASURE.

Come, and feast thy ravish'd sight
In the regions of delight;
Bacchus in his rosy bower,
Waits to crown the festive hour;
Lovely with attractive charms,
Venus wooes thee to her arms:
Haste thee, gentle youth, and prove
The sweets of liberty and love.

CATCH.

1st Gambler. Pass the box.
2d G. Come, pass it faster.
Groom Porter. Seven the hazard, four the caster!
3d G. The odds!—two hundred here to one!
Caster. With you, sir!
3d G. Done!
Caster. And you, sir!
4th G. Done!
5th G. Come, cover, cover.
6th G. Set about.
Cast. Here goes—here goes.
Groom Porter. The Caster's out.

CHO-

CHORUS.

(The one half singing the two first lines—the others the last.)

Eight hundred gone! that hellish sice!
Such luck! O curse the box and dice!

Eight hundred gain'd! that lucky sice!
Well done! well done! good box and dice!

Groom P.   The box is your's, sir.
1st G.   Come, the main.
Groom.   A seven.
2d G.   Fifty!
Caster.   Done!
3d G.   Again.
4th G.   Five hundred!
Caster.   Done!
6th G.   Again!
Cast.   With you.
6th G.   I've lost a thousand.
1st G.   I've lost two.
   I'll try again, whate'er befal,
   A thousand!
Caster.   Done, I set ye all.
2d G.   Throw, throw.
3d G.   Ay, now the sport begins.
Cast.   Here goes.
Groom.   A nick; the Caster wins.

CHO-

CHORUS *(as before.)*

Four thousand pounds! that hellish sice!
Such luck! O damn the box and dice!

Four thousand gain'd! that lucky sice!
Well done, well done, good box and dice!

SONG.

BRIDEWELL-KEEPER.

Ye Scamps, ye Pads, ye Divers, and all upon
    the lay,
In Tothill fields gay sheep-walk like lambs ye
    sport and play,
Rattling up your darbies, come hither at my
    call,
I'm Jigger Dubber here, and you're welcome to
    Mill Doll.

With my tow row, &c.

At your insurance-office the Flats you've taken in;
The game you've play'd, my Kiddy, you're always sure to win;
First you touch the Shiners—the number up—you break,
With your insuring policy! I'd not insure your neck.

The French with trotters nimble, could fly from English blows,
And they've got nimble daddles, as Monsieur plainly shews:
Be thus the foes of Britain bang'd, ay thump away Monsieur,
The hemp you're beating now, will make your solitaire.

My peepers, who've we here now! why this is sure Black Moll;
My ma'am you're of the fair sex, so welcome to Mill Doll:
The cull with you who'd venture into a snoozing ken,
Like blackamoor Othello, should put out the light, and then——

I think,

I think, my flashy coachman, that you'll take
    better care,
Not for a little bub come the flang upon your
    fare:
Your jazy pays the garnish, unless the fees you
    tip,
Tho' you're a flashy coachman, here the gagger
    holds the whip.

CHORUS.

We're scamps, we're pads, we're divers, we're all
    upon the lay,
In Tothill-fields gay sheep-walk like lambs we
    sport and play;
Rattling up our darbies, we're hither at your call,
You are Jigger Dubber here, and we're forc'd
    for to mill doll.

With our tow row, &c.

PART

PART II.

RECITATIVE.

VIRTUE.

At length, repentant youth, with joy I see,
Misled by pleasure, thou return'st to me,
Henceforth my steps if thou pursue,
And keep me ever in thy view.

AIR.

Smiling Fortune shall befriend thee,
Hymen's joys shall still attend thee;
Every blessing thou shalt know,
Which Peace and Virtue can bestow.

SCENE—*A Prison.*

AIR.

FIRST PRISONER.

Alas, sir, I fear we are in for our lives.

SECOND PRISONER.

For stealing three shillings.

THIRD PRISONER.

For marrying three wives.
A pious old Doctor has shewn me the way,
And has brought me to this by his *Thelyphthora.*

Chorus. Could you knock off, &c.

FOURTH PRISONER.

I lent my friend money, and lo, in the end,
Too common a case, lost both money and friend;
For prudently *he* made the best of his way,
And kindly has left me the reck'ning to pay.

FIFTH PRISONER.

Would you think it? an impudent harlot has
  swore,
That I made her by force,—what she was long
  before;
And unless some good friend gets me out of the
  scrape,
'Tis a hundred to one but I'm hang'd for a rape.

SIXTH PRISONER.

Behold a poor bard, an unfortunate wight,
Whose piece was unluckily damn'd the first night;
When my butcher and taylor were rather severe,
And have sent me to finish my tragedy *here*.

CHORUS.

Then knock off our chains, sir, on this happy day,
And your humble petitioners ever shall pray.

SONG.
MIDSHIPMAN.

Come, my boys, let us go, since again we are free;
Let us haste to the empire of freedom, the sea,
Where each proud usurper we'll boldly dethrone,
And tell 'em that kingdom was always our own.
We owe the French something for tricks t'other day,
The debt of a drubbing, which gladly we'll pay;
Their bravadoes we'll scorn, and their threats we despise,
We yield but to conquer, and sink but to rise;
With Parker and Rodney, we'll trim the Mounseers,
We'll tickle the Spaniards, and wing the Mynheers.

II.

One William preserv'd our religion and laws,
And another now rises to plead our great cause,
This brave, gallant youth, is a true Britain born,
His King he'll defend, and his country adorn.
Each hardship, each danger, he'll boldly defy,
For Digby shall teach him to conquer or die.
Tho' the waves have been rough, and the wind in our teeth,
We smile at misfortune, wounds, shipwreck and death;
And still hope, my dear boys, that by shifting our sail,
At last we shall meet with a prosperous gale.

RECITATIVE.

VIRTUE.

Thanks, noble youth, thy debt of honor's paid,
My voice is heard, and my commands obey'd;
My laws thou hast observ'd with due regard,
And soon shalt thou receive the bright reward.

Safe in the arms of beauty's Queen,
Transported to the blissful scene,
Where fortune first indulgent smil'd,
And bleft with wealth her darling child;
There shall the nuptial knot be ty'd,
In all the pomp of eastern pride.

SONG.

LIEUTENANT.

As you mean to set sail for the land of delight,
And in wedlock's soft hammocks to swing e'very
  night,
If you hope that your voyage succesful shou'd
  prove,
Fill your sails with affection, your cabbin with
  love.   *Fill your sails, &c.*

Let your heart, like the main-mast, be ever
  upright,
And the Union you boast, like our tackle be
  tight;
Of the shoals of Indiff'rence be sure to keep
  clear,
And the quicksands of jealousy never come near.
          And the, &c.

If husbands e'er hope to live peaceable lives,
They must reckon themselves, give the helm
    to their wives;
For the evener we go, boys, the better we sail,
And on ship board the helm is still rul'd by the
    tail.
        And on shipboard, &c.

Then list to your pilot, my boy, and be wise;
If my precepts you scorn, and my maxims de-
    spise,
A brace of proud antlers your brows may
    adorn;
And a hundred to one but you double Cape
    Horn.

RECITATIVE.

PLEASURE.

All-subduing goddess, see,
Pleasure comes to join with thee.

VIRTUE.

Then let us join the social lay,
And celebrate this happy day.

EPITHALAMIUM.

VIRTUE.

Her choicest gifts with lavish hand,
See, smiling plenty pours,
Whilst peace, at Hymen's soft command,
Lights up the chearful hours.

Still shall each fresh returning spring
Its earliest roses shed,
And Flora all her tribute bring,
To strew the nuptial bed.

PLEA-

PLEASURE.

Brisk youth, exulting god, shalt lead
His fair attendant, joy,
To crown with bliss his best lov'd
maid,
And grace his favorite boy.

Whilst the gay nymph and jocund
swain
In festal chorus move,
And Venus joins the sportive train
With harmony and love.

CHORUS.

Thus let us join the social lay,
And celebrate this happy day;
The bands which vice and folly weave,
Soon will loosen and deceive.

Virtue's adamantine chain
Still unbroken shall remain.

GENERAL CHORUS.

Happy must the union prove,
Form'd by virtue and by love.

THE PROCESSION.

Printed by Libri Plureos GmbH in Hamburg, Germany